# Food from Farmers

# BREAD!

## Life on a Wheat Farm

by Ruth Owen

WINDMILL
BOOKS

New York

Published in 2012 by Windmill Books, an Imprint of Rosen Publishing
29 East 21st Street, New York, NY 10010

Editor for Ruby Tuesday Books Ltd: Mark J. Sachner
U.S. Editor: Julia Quinlan
Designer: Emma Randall
Consultant: Logan Peterman, Laughing Sprout Family Farm

Photo Credits: Cover, 1, 4–5, 6–7, 8–9, 10–11, 12–13, 14–15, 16–17, 19, 20–21, 23, 25 (center), 26 (top left), 26 (center left), 27, 28–29, 30–31 © Shutterstock; 18 © Superstock; 22 © Wikipedia Creative Commons (public domain); 23 (top) © Getty Images; 24 © Alamy; 26 (bottom left), 26 (bottom right) © istock.

Library of Congress Cataloging-in-Publication Data

Owen, Ruth, 1967–
 Bread! : life on a wheat farm / by Ruth Owen.
   p. cm. — (Food from farmers)
 Life on a wheat farm
 Includes index.
 ISBN 978-1-61533-532-9 (library binding) — ISBN 978-1-61533-544-2 (pbk.) —
ISBN 978-1-61533-545-9 (6-pack)
 1. Wheat—Juvenile literature. 2. Farm life—Juvenile literature. I. Title. II. Title: Life on a wheat farm. III. Series: Food from farmers.
 SB191.W5O84 2012
 633.1'1—dc23

                              2011028928

Manufactured in the United States of America

CPSIA Compliance Information: Batch #BOW2102WM: For Further Information contact Windmill Books, New York, New York at 1-866-478-0556

# CONTENTS

# WELCOME TO MY FARM!

Hi! My name is Elliott. I am 12 years old. I live on a farm with my dad, uncle, aunt, and two grown-up cousins.

We grow wheat on our farm. Our farm is an **organic** farm. We grow our **crops** in a way that is kind to planet Earth.

Dad

Our farm is in North Dakota. There are over 19,000 wheat farms in this state. In fact, about one-quarter of North Dakota is covered by wheat fields!

Wheat is used to make flour.
Most people eat foods that contain wheat flour every day!

Breakfast bagel

Lunchtime sandwich

Spaghetti for dinner

Snacks

## WILL'S WHEAT FARM FACTS

- **Wheat farmers in the United States grow more wheat than Americans eat. About half the wheat grown in the U.S. is sold to 100 different countries around the world.**

# LET'S LOOK AROUND THE FARM

## This is a map of our farm.

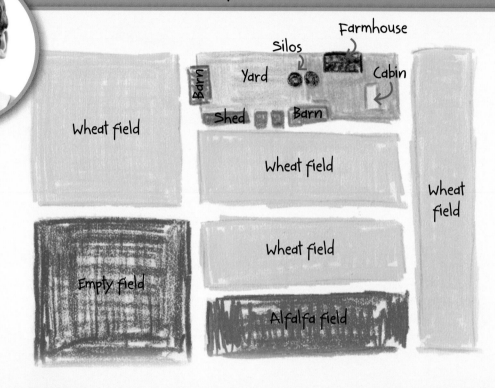

Farmhouse

Silos

Barn

Yard

Cabin

Shed

Barn

Wheat field

Wheat field

Wheat field

Empty field

Wheat field

Alfalfa field

Dad and I live in the cabin.
My uncle's family lives in
the farmhouse.

Our cabin

Our farm covers nearly 1,500 **acres** (607 ha) of land.
An acre is a measurement used to measure farms.
An acre is just a little smaller than a football field.

Different types of wheat are grown to make different foods.

We grow hard red spring wheat on our farm.
Hard wheats are used to make foods such as bread, rolls,
bagels, and pizza crust.

We also grow durum wheat. This type of wheat is used to
make pasta, such as spaghetti and macaroni.

Uncle
Richard

### WILL'S WHEAT FARM FACTS

- Each year, North Dakota produces enough wheat to make 14 billion loaves of bread and nearly 14 billion servings of spaghetti!

Durum wheat

# ALL ABOUT WHEAT

Wheat is a type of grain. A grain is a grass plant that produces seeds, which people eat. Oats, corn, rice, rye, barley, millet, and sorghum are also grains.

Inside the wheat plant's head are the kernels. Each wheat head has about 50 kernels.

Head

Kernels

Leaf

Stem

This is a close-up drawing of a tiny wheat kernel.

**ENDOSPERM**
The endosperm is the part that is used to make white flour.

**BRAN**
The bran is the hard, outer part of the kernel. It is made up of many layers.

**GERM**
The germ is the seed. This is the part that grows into a new wheat plant.

# TIME TO PLANT THE WHEAT

We plant our wheat in April or May when the soil gets warm. Warm soil helps the wheat seeds start to grow. Dad, Uncle Richard, and my cousins get the fields ready.

The tractor pulls a cultivator through the soil. The cultivator destroys any young **weeds** that are ready to grow in the soil.

My cousin, Chris

Cultivator

Soil

## WILL'S WHEAT FACTS

• Weeds may block sunlight from reaching the wheat plants. Weeds also use up water and **nutrients** that the wheat plants need.

Next, we put a grain drill onto the tractor.
The drill is used to plant the wheat seeds.
The drill digs a channel in the soil and drops in the seeds.
Then it covers the seeds with soil.

Grain drill

The wheat soon starts to grow.

# GROWING THE ORGANIC WAY

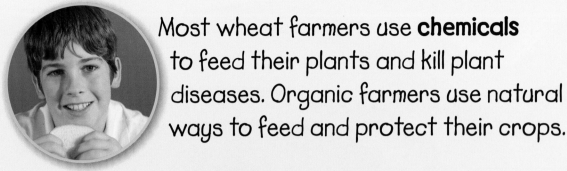

Most wheat farmers use **chemicals** to feed their plants and kill plant diseases. Organic farmers use natural ways to feed and protect their crops.

This farmer is spraying chemicals on his crops.

Chemicals can make insects, birds, and other wild animals sick.
We feed our wheat with **manure** from our neighbor's cattle farm!
We spread the manure on the fields.
The manure is filled with nutrients that our plants need.

Manure

We also grow crops such as clover and alfalfa.
These crops are known as green manure.
We plow up these crops and mix them into the soil.
The plants rot and make nutrients for our wheat!

Field of alfalfa

## WILL'S WHEAT FARM FACTS

- A wheat disease may stay in the soil in a wheat field. Organic farmers trick the disease by leaving the field empty for a year. They may also grow a different crop there for one year. With no wheat to attack, the disease dies out!

# THE WHEAT CROP

The wheat plants grow and grow.
They can grow as high as four feet (1.2m) tall.

Wheat farmers have plenty to worry about. High winds or hailstorms can flatten and ruin a crop. Wheat needs water to grow. If we don't get enough rain, the wheat won't grow well.

Dry soil

A field of dry wheat may even catch fire if the weather is too hot!

At first the wheat is green. Then, in July, the green plants start to turn golden. It is nearly time to **harvest** the wheat.

Now, Dad and Uncle Richard want the weather to stay dry. The wheat must be dry so that it can be stored. Wet or damp wheat will spoil when it is kept in storage bins.

## WILL'S WHEAT FARM FACTS

- **Wheat was first planted in the United States in 1777.**

# HARVEST TIME

Our harvest time in North Dakota usually begins in August.

Dad tests the wheat by chewing some kernels. If the kernels are hard but turn gum-like in his mouth, the wheat is ripe. Farmers have tested wheat this way for hundreds of years!

A huge machine called a combine harvester cuts the wheat. Then it separates the stems, leaves, and dry pieces, called chaff, from the kernels.

Combine harvester

The combine harvester collects the kernels and empties them into a truck.

Wheat kernels

17

# SELLING THE WHEAT

The trucks take the wheat to a place known as the elevator.

At the elevator, the grain is put into large, metal storage bins called silos. The silos look like towers.

At the elevator, our grain is weighed. The workers also check its **quality** and give the wheat a grade. It's like getting a grade for your schoolwork. The higher the grade, the more the elevator pays Dad for the wheat.

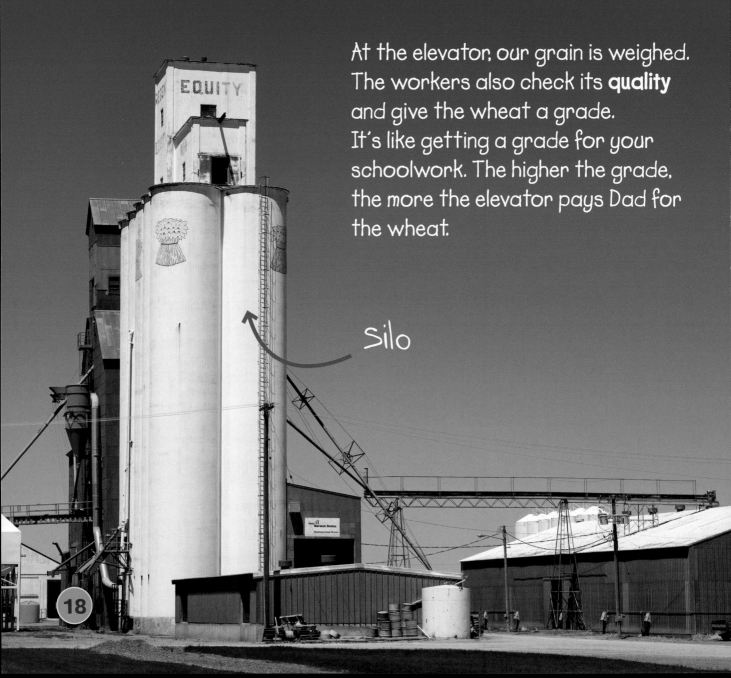

Silo

Wheat is bought and sold using a measurement called a bushel. A bushel of wheat kernels weighs 60 pounds (27 kg).

One acre of wheatfield can produce 42 bushels of wheat.

## WILL'S WHEAT FACTS

- A bushel of wheat can be made into 43 pounds (19.5 kg) of white flour. That's enough flour to make bread for 504 sandwiches!

# A DAY IN THE LIFE OF A FARM

At harvest time, Dad, Uncle Richard, and my cousins work from early morning until late in the evening.

**6:00 a.m.**
Everybody meets at the farmhouse for coffee and lots of toast!

**7:00 a.m.**
Dad and Uncle Richard drive the combines out into the fields. The harvest is underway!

## WILL'S WHEAT FACTS

- A pound of wheat kernels contains up to 17,000 tiny kernels!

**9:00 a.m.**
My cousins race to the elevator with trucks of grain.

**12:00 p.m.**
Acre after acre of wheat is cut.

Baling machine

**3:00 p.m.**
My cousin uses a baling machine to turn the wheat stalks into bales of straw. We sell the straw for animal bedding.

Straw bale

**5:00 p.m.**
No time to rest, because it looks like rain!

**9:00 p.m.**
It's finally time for supper. Aunt Caroline has made ravioli.

I wonder if the ravioli was made from our durum wheat!

# MILLING THE WHEAT

The wheat kernels are taken from the elevator to a mill. A mill is a **processing plant** where the grain is made into flour.

At the mill, the grain moves through a number of milling machines.

Milling machine

Inside the machines are large steel rollers—like giant rolling pins!

The rollers crush the kernels.

The bran and germ break off from the kernels. The endosperm is ground into small pieces called semolina.

Endosperm

Bran

Germ

Inside this machine, the semolina is sifted to separate it from the bits of bran and germ.

Sifting machine

Then the semolina goes back into the milling machines to be ground into powdery white flour

White flour

Semolina

The flour is packed into bags to go to supermarkets and grocery stores. It is loaded into tanker trucks to go to bakeries.

SELF-RISING
ENRICHED
*Flour*
BLEACHED

NET WT 5 LB (2.26 kg)

## WILL'S WHEAT FACTS

- **Whole wheat flour is made by grinding the whole wheat kernel. The flour includes the bran, endosperm, and germ.**

# HOW IS BREAD MADE?

At a bakery, or bread factory, flour is mixed with water and yeast to make dough. Yeast is a type of **fungus**.

The dough is mixed in a mixing machine.

Mixing machine

This is a huge piece of dough!

## WILL'S BREAD FACTS

- When yeast is mixed with flour and water, it makes thousands of tiny air bubbles. The air bubbles make the dough get bigger, or rise. The bubbles also make the bread light and fluffy to chew.

A machine cuts the dough into small pieces. The pieces move along a conveyor belt. Machines fold and roll the dough into shapes.

Conveyor belt

The pieces of dough sit in a hot area called the proofer for an hour so that they rise. Then they are baked in ovens.

Oven

Sometimes dough is baked in molds to give the loaves a special shape.

# HOW IS PASTA MADE?

Durum wheat kernels go to a mill to be ground up into semolina.

At a pasta factory, semolina is mixed with water to make pasta dough.

Cutters called dies are used to make the dough into pasta shapes. Different dies make different shapes.

Pasta dough

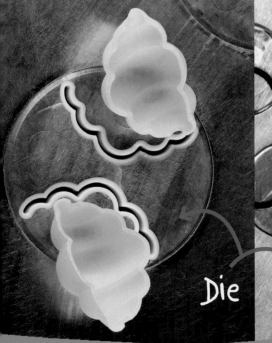

Die

The pasta dough is forced through the die. Then the pasta is dried.

This machine is cutting and filling pieces of ravioli.

When the pasta is dry, it is packaged into bags and boxes. Now it's ready to be sold in grocery stores and supermarkets.

## WILL'S PASTA FACTS

- Each adult in the United States eats about 15.5 pounds (7 kg) of pasta each year!

# WE LOVE BREAD!

I love to eat freshly baked bread. It's very good for my body, too!

Foods that contain wheat, such as bread and pasta, contain complex **carbohydrates**.

Complex carbohydrates give our bodies the energy to play, work, and do sports.

Eating **whole wheat bread** made from the whole grain keeps our hearts healthy. The bran part of the wheat gives us **fiber**. Fiber keeps our **digestive systems** working well.

- Wheat contains iron and B **vitamins**. These nutrients give the body energy. Your blood needs iron to help it carry oxygen around your body.

These are my favorite ways to get my wheat goodness.

Toast with peanut butter

Fajitas made with wheat tortillas

Macaroni and cheese

Thank you to wheat farmers everywhere!

# GLOSSARY

**acre (AY-ker)**
A unit of measurement used for measuring land, especially on farms.

**carbohydrates (kar-boh-HY-drayts)**
The main element in foods made mostly from plants, such as potatoes and bread.

**chemicals (KEH-mih-kulz)**
Matter that can be mixed with other matter to cause changes.

**crops (KRAHPS)**
Plants that are grown in large quantities on a farm.

**digestive system (dy-JES-tiv SIS-tem)**
The group of body parts, such as the stomach, that break down food so that a body can use it for fuel.

**fiber (FY-ber)**
Material found in plants. Your body can't break down fiber, so it pushes it through your digestive system, which helps keep your poop moving out of your body.

**fungi (FUN-jy)**
A member of a group of living things, called fungi, that are not plants or animals. Mushrooms are a type of fungus.

**harvest (HAR-vist)**
To gather, cut, pick, or dig up crops when they are ripe.

**manure (muh-NOOR)**
Animal waste.

**nutrients (NOO-tree-ents)**
Substances that the body needs to help it live and grow. Foods contain nutrients such as vitamins.

**organic farm (or-GA-nik FARN)**
A farm that doesn't use chemicals to feed crops or to kill weeds, diseases, and insects that eat or damage crops. Organic farms are kinder to planet Earth.

**processing plant (PRAH-ses-ing PLANT)**
A place, like a factory, where a series of actions are carried out to prepare or change something.

**quality (KWAH-luh-tee)**
How good something is.

**ripe (RYP)**
Fully grown and ready to be picked or eaten.

**vitamin (VY-tuh-min)**
A substance found in foods that is needed by the body for health and growth.

**weed (WEED)**
A plant growing where it is not wanted. Weeds are often tough, wild plants that grow very quickly.

**whole wheat bread (HOHL HWEET BRED)**
Bread made from whole wheat flour. This type of flour is made by grinding up the whole wheat kernel so the flour contains the bran, endosperm, and germ.

# WEB SITES

For Web resources related to the subject of this book,
go to: www.windmillbooks.com/weblinks
and select this book's title.

# READ MORE

Blake, Susannah. *Bread & Pizzas. Make and Eat.* New York: PowerKids Press, 2009.

Thoennes Keller, Kristen. *From Wheat to Bread. First Facts*: From Farm to Table. Minnesota: Capstone Press, 2004.

Levenson, George. *Bread Comes to Life: A Garden of Wheat and a Load to Eat.* New York: Tricycle Press, 2008

# INDEX